ALL ABOUT FANTASY CREATURES

Discover
ORCS,
BOGGARTS
AND
Other Nasty
Fantasy Creatures

A.J. Sautter

raintree

a Capstone company — publisher

Raintree is an imprint of Capstone Global Library Limited, a company incorporated in England and Wales having its registered office at 264 Banbury Road, Oxford, OX2 7DY – Registered company number: 6695582

www.raintree.co.uk
myorders@raintree.co.uk

Edited by Adrian Vigliano
Designed by Bobbie Nuytten
Picture research by Wanda Winch
Production by Laura Manthe
Originated by Capstone Global Library
Printed and bound in China

ISBN 978 1 4747 4256 6
21 20 19 18 17
10 9 8 7 6 5 4 3 2 1

British Library Cataloguing in Publication Data
A full catalogue record for this book is available from the British Library.

Acknowledgements
We would like to thank the following for permission to reproduce photographs: Capstone: Colin Ashcroft, 4, 28, Collin Howard, 17, 25, 27, Jason Juta, 3, 19, 21, Martin Bustamante, cover (bottom left, right), 1 (right), 7, 9, 11, 13, Stefano Azzalin, 5, 32, Tom McGrath, 15, 23; Shutterstock: Carlos Caetano, cover (background), 1 (background).

Every effort has been made to contact copyright holders of material reproduced in this book. Any omissions will be rectified in subsequent printings if notice is given to the publisher.

CONTENTS

NASTY FANTASY CREATURES!

Fantasy tales feature many nasty creatures. Wicked orcs, hags and others cause a lot of trouble for heroes. What would these creatures be like if they were real? Where and how would they live? Let's look deeper to find out!

Fact: People long ago believed that fantasy creatures were real. When mysterious things happened, they often blamed it on wicked fantasy creatures.

BLACK ORCS

Size: 2 to 2.1 metres (6.5 to 7 feet) tall

Home: mountain caves or strong fortresses

Diet: rats, mountain goats, dwarves, humans

Lifespan: unknown

Appearance: Black orcs are big and strong. Their tough skin is often marked with battle scars. They have yellow eyes, pointed ears and greasy black hair. Their mouths are full of jagged teeth and fangs.

crossbow type of bow that is held and fired with a trigger like a gun

catapult weapon used to hurl large rocks or other objects at enemies

Behaviour: Evil wizards grow black orcs in special underground chambers. These creatures are violent, cruel and short-tempered. Black orcs are highly skilled warriors. They often use complex weapons, such as **crossbows** and **catapults**.

BOGGARTS

Size: 20 to 30 centimetres (8 to 12 inches) tall
Home: cupboards, attics and other small spaces in old houses
Diet: stale bread, sour milk, mouldy cheese, old food scraps
Lifespan: unknown

Appearance: Boggarts are a wicked form of brownies. They are bigger and stronger than brownies and have green skin. They have black eyes, pointed ears and coarse whiskers. A boggart's mouth is full of nasty, sharp teeth.

Behaviour: Brownies turn into nasty boggarts if they become angry. Boggarts never kill. They do enjoy breaking things, playing pranks and causing problems. Anyone who insults a boggart should apologize. It will then return to its friendly brownie form.

GOBLINS

Size: 1.2 to 1.4 metres (4 to 4.5 ft) tall
Home: deep, dark mountain caves
Diet: worms, insects, mushrooms, rats, gnomes
Lifespan: 20 to 25 years

Appearance: Goblins are often mistaken for orcs. However, they are smaller and usually walk in a bent over position. Goblins have pointed ears, large yellow eyes and sharp, jagged teeth.

Behaviour: Goblins never leave their dark caves during the day. They don't produce their own food. They instead **raid** farms and villages for what they need. However, goblins often create clever traps and weapons to defend their homes.

raid make a sudden, surprise attack on a place

GREMLINS

Size: 0.6 to 0.8 metres (2 to 2.5 ft) tall
Home: deep, dark underground caves
Diet: worms, insects, snails, salamanders
Lifespan: 5 to 6 years

Appearance: Gremlins usually have scaly green skin. Their large eyes are often blue, but can be yellow, green or red. They have jagged teeth and long, sharp **talons**. Their huge ears are shaped like a bat's wings.

talon long, sharp claw

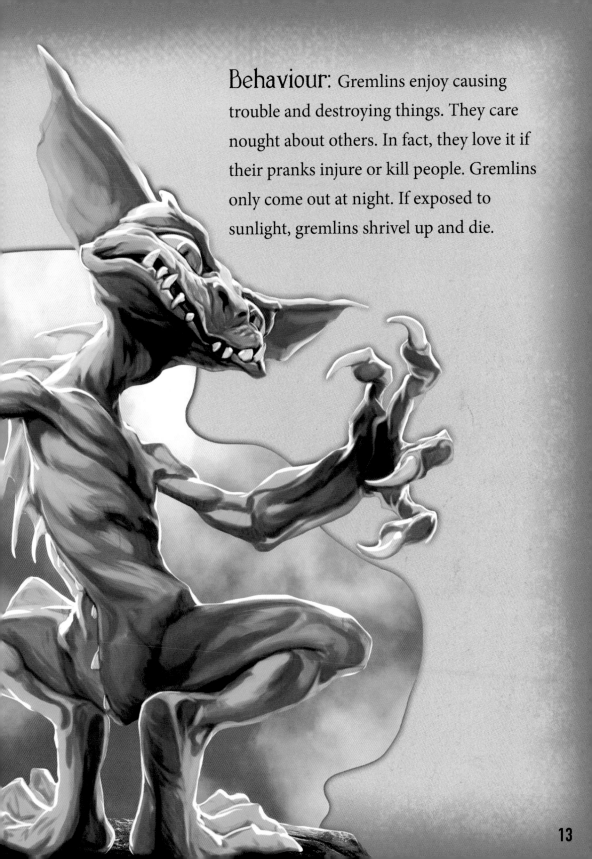

Behaviour: Gremlins enjoy causing trouble and destroying things. They care nought about others. In fact, they love it if their pranks injure or kill people. Gremlins only come out at night. If exposed to sunlight, gremlins shrivel up and die.

Hags

Size: 1.7 to 1.8 metres (5.5 to 6 ft) tall

Home: damp caves or ruined old shacks

Diet: worms, snails, slugs, toads, rats, humans

Lifespan: unknown

Appearance: Hags look like hideous old women. They have thin bodies, hunched backs and stringy hair. Their green skin is often covered in hairy warts. They have long pointed noses and black, rotting teeth.

lair hideout used by wicked people to keep their activities secret

Behaviour: Hags affect the lands where they live. Forests and wetlands become dead and rotten. Hags have a strong craving for human flesh. They use magic spells to lure people into their dark **lairs**. There they can satisfy their hunger.

Hobgoblins

Size: 1.7 to 1.8 metres (5.5 to 6 ft) tall

Home: mountain caves or ruined stone castles

Diet: rabbits, sheep, goats, gnomes, goblins, dwarves

Lifespan: about 35 years

Appearance: Hobgoblins are covered in coarse brown or black hair. Most have red eyes and two sharp tusks in their lower jaws. Many hobgoblins wear bits of bone or metal in their beards.

Behaviour: Hobgoblins value military training. Children begin training as soon as they can hold a sword. Hobgoblins often use complex weapons like crossbows. They are tireless fighters. During battles, they keep fighting until they win or are killed.

NIXIES

Size: 1.2 to 1.4 metres (4 to 4.5 ft) tall

Home: warm freshwater ponds and lakes

Diet: fish, clams, frogs, water plants

Lifespan: unknown, possibly up to 400 years

Appearance: Nixies hatch from eggs and grow like tadpoles. Their arms, legs and flipper-like feet grow out as they get older. Nixies have pale green skin covered with fish-like scales. Instead of ears, nixies have **gills** to breathe underwater.

> **gill** body part used to breathe underwater
>
> **illusion** something that appears to be real but isn't

Behaviour: Nixies normally use **illusions** to keep people away from their homes. However, some nixies are more wicked. They use their magic to trap people and use them as slaves.

Orcs

Size: 1.4 to 1.5 metres (4.5 to 5 ft) tall
Home: mountain caves and deserted castles
Diet: rats, squirrels, rabbits, deer, humans, elves
Lifespan: about 50 years

Appearance: Orcs can have black, brown, grey or white skin. Some have long, greasy hair. Others have no hair at all. Most orcs are ugly and have squinty eyes, pointed ears and jagged teeth.

Behaviour: Orcs hate nature and beautiful artwork. They hate elves most of all. Orcs are related to black orcs, but are shorter and weaker. They are cruel and have violent tempers. Orcs are also not very clever. However, they do often make clever weapons and armour from wood and bone.

PIXIES

Size: 15 to 20 cm (6 to 8 in) tall

Home: hollow trees and logs

Diet: seeds, nuts, wild berries, mushrooms, honey

Lifespan: about 300 years

Appearance: Pixies look similar to small fairies. Pixies have large eyes, pointed ears and butterfly-like wings. They usually have black or dark brown hair. Their clothing is often made from dead leaves or grass.

Behaviour: Pixies like to explore the world. They enjoy stealing small items like thimbles, toothpicks and string. Pixies enjoy playing tricks on people, but their pranks often go too far. People sometimes get hurt.

SIRENS

Size: 1.8 to 2 metres (6 to 6.5 ft) long

Home: rocky islands and ocean coastlines

Diet: fish, oysters, sea urchins, starfish, octopuses, human sailors

Lifespan: up to 1,000 years

Appearance: Sirens look like monstrous mermaids. They have scaly yellow-green skin and clawed hands. Their fins are often red or blue. Sirens have sharp, needle-like teeth. They use their strong tails for fast swimming.

prey animal hunted by another animal for food

Behaviour: Sirens are also known as sea hags. They use magic to trick sailors at sea. Sailors believe the sirens are beautiful women calling from shore. The sailors often smash their ships on nearby rocks. Then sirens can easily capture their foolish **prey**.

TROGLODYTES

Size: 1.5 to 1.7 metres (5 to 5.5 ft) tall

Home: damp, underground caves or dark swamps

Diet: fish, frogs, snakes, birds, muskrats, humans

Lifespan: up to 130 years

Appearance: Most troglodytes have scaly green skin. Their jaws are filled with razor-sharp teeth. They have powerful tails like an alligator's. Males have colourful **frills** on their heads and necks. Some people think troglodytes are a type of **humanoid** dragon.

frill flap of skin on a reptile's head or neck

humanoid shaped somewhat like a human

sacrifice something valuable that is offered to a god; often a living creature is killed to honour the god

Behaviour: Troglodytes are strong and fierce fighters. They often raid villages to steal food, weapons, treasure and people. Captives are used as slaves, food or **sacrifices** to the Troglodytes' gods.

Creature quiz

1. Which of the following do orcs hate the most?

   A) gnomes

   B) elves

   C) pixies

2. If you're on a ship and see a beautiful woman singing and waving to you from shore, it is probably a:

   A) siren.

   B) nixie.

   C) gorgon.

3. Gremlins are best known for:

   A) creating clever weapons and traps.

   B) playing pranks and destroying things.

   C) raiding villages to steal food.

4. The best way to deal with a troublesome boggart is to:

   A) expose it to sunlight.

   B) offer it money to leave you alone.

   C) apologize for any insults.

5. Troglodytes often raid villages to steal:

   A) food and weapons.

   B) treasure and people.

   C) all of the above.

6. Which wicked creatures make the best warriors?

   A) goblins
   B) black orcs
   C) troglodytes

7. How do hags catch their victims?

   A) They use magic to lure people into their homes.
   B) They steal children during the night.
   C) They use a magic sleeping potion.

8. How are black orcs created?

   A) They are born as babies.
   B) They are made magically.
   C) They are grown underground in special chambers.

9. As nixies age, they grow:

   A) fins and tails like a fish.
   B) legs, arms and feet like a tadpole.
   C) claws like a crab or lobster.

10. As pixies explore the world they like to:

   A) collect small trinkets like toothpicks and thimbles.
   B) play pranks on people for fun.
   C) both A and B.

See page 31 for quiz answers.

Glossary

catapult   weapon used to hurl large rocks or other objects at enemies

crossbow   type of bow that is held and fired with a trigger like a gun

frill   flap of skin on a reptile's head or neck

gill   body part used to breathe underwater

humanoid   shaped somewhat like a human

illusion   something that appears to be real but isn't

lair   hideout used by wicked people to keep their activities secret

prey   animal hunted by another animal for food

raid   make a sudden, surprise attack on a place

sacrifice   something valuable that is offered to a god; often a living creature is killed to honour the god

talon   long, sharp claw

Find out more

Books

Hansel and Gretel (Stories Around the World), Cari Meister (Raintree, 2016)

How to Draw Orcs, Goblins and Other Wicked Creatures (Drawing Fantasy Creatures), A.J. Sautter (Capstone Press, 2016)

Quiz answers:

1:B, 2:A, 3:B, 4:C, 5:C, 6:B, 7:A, 8:C, 9:B, 10:C

Website

mocomi.com/mythical-creatures-part-1

Find out more about mythical creatures on this website.

Index